ANIMALS NEED FOOD

MARLA CONN

Photo Glossary

 bear

 bug

 carrot

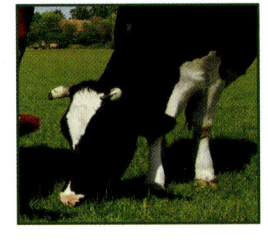 cow

 fish

 frog

 fruit

 grass

 nuts

 people

 rabbit

 squirrel

High Frequency Words:
- a
- food
- to
- animals
- live
- will
- eat
- need

Animals need food to live.

Animals need food to live.

bear

A **bear** will eat a **fish**.

Animals need food to live.

frog

Animals need food to live.

grass

Animals need food to live.

people

Activity

1. Go back and read the story with a partner.

2. Discuss the different kinds of food that different animals eat.

3. Why do you think animals need to eat?

> **Teacher read-aloud:**
> *Food provides our body with nutrients. Nutrients give us energy to be active, to grow, and to keep our bodies healthy. We need nutrients to breathe, to eat, to keep warm, and to heal when we get sick.*

4. Why is it important to eat a healthy diet?

5. Plan a healthy menu for the day. Include breakfast, lunch, dinner, and two snacks. Don't forget water! Share your healthy menu with classmates.